# MY FUN WITH
# READING

◆

*Stories About*
*Plants*

# MY FUN WITH
# READING

## BOOK 2

*Stories About Plants*

SERIES EDITOR
### Ronald Kidd

READING CONSULTANTS
### Paul E. Stanton, Ph.D.
*University of South Carolina, Coastal Carolina College*

### Ann Lukasevich, Ed.D.
*University of British Columbia*

THE SOUTHWESTERN COMPANY ■ NASHVILLE, TENNESSEE

RONALD KIDD is owner and Editorial Director of Kidd & Company, Inc., a Nashville-based packager and producer of children's books and records. Previously he held positions as Creative Director, Walt Disney Records, and Editor, Bowmar/Noble Publishers. The published author of seventeen books, he was recipient of the Children's Choice Award, the CINE Golden Eagle, and two Gold Records. He has been nominated for the Edgar Allan Poe Award, the Grammy Award, and the California Young Reader Medal. Mr. Kidd has a secondary teaching credential in English and history.

DR. PAUL E. STANTON completed his Ph.D. at the University of South Carolina in the field of Counseling Psychology, with an emphasis in reading and learning disabilities. He chaired the Department of Reading and Language Arts at the University of Pittsburgh and was co-chair of the Committee on Undergraduate Training in the Teaching of Reading for the International Reading Association (IRA). He was co-developer of the Scholastic *Action* Series, a pioneer high-interest/low-ability reading series produced by Scholastic Book Services. Dr. Stanton served as Vice Chancellor for Academic Affairs at the University of South Carolina, Coastal Carolina College, where he is currently Professor of Psychology specializing in reading and learning disabilities.

DR. ANN LUKASEVICH taught for seventeen years at the elementary school level in Ontario, Canada. She is presently a member of the Language Department at the University of British Columbia, where she originally obtained her Ed.D., and teaches courses in language, reading, early childhood, and curriculum development. She also taught reading and language courses at the University of Calgary for one year and at the University of Western Ontario for three years. During this period, she has done numerous workshops and conference presentations in early childhood education, reading, and language in Canada and the United States. She spent a year in Britain studying British education, and was awarded an advanced Diploma in Child Development. Her interests include parent involvement, evaluation, literacy development, and computer education.

SERIES DESIGN      Bruce Gore
PAGE DESIGN AND ART PRODUCTION      Schatz + Schatz
COVER PHOTOS      David Cavagnaro (top)
                  Stephen McBrady (center and bottom)

# CONTENTS

# SEEDS
## *That Travel*

by YVONNE MARTIN

*If you need help*
*with hard words,*
*please turn to p. 36.*

PHOTOGRAPHS: David Cavagnaro
ILLUSTRATIONS: Joel Snyder
BOTANICAL CONSULTANT: David Cavagnaro

Imagine this.

Imagine that you are strolling through the countryside on a sunny spring day. In a field, the grass is so high it reaches your waist. At the edge of the clearing is a stand of lush, green trees.

You stop to rest and admire the pretty wildflowers dotting the field. As you lie still, a breeze cools the air. Everything seems fresh and alive.

Farther on, you discover a pond. Its still surface reflects the afternoon sun.

Now stop. Have a seat. And think.

Where did these flowers, plants, and trees come from? How did they get here?

If you look hard enough, you will find the answer. You can see nature at work planting the field. Seeds are on the move, carried by the breeze, by squirrels and birds, by a gently flowing stream. They are looking for a place to call home.

Like people, seeds come in many sizes, shapes, and colors. Some, such as orchid seeds, are as small as bits of dust. Others are quite large. The seeds of a double-coconut plant can be as big as a basketball!

*Chipmunk*

*Double-coconut seeds*

*Coast live oak*

Seeds come in many colors — yellow, red, green, brown, pink, black. Some are round, and others are shaped like eggs. Many seeds have shapes that are simply too hard to describe.

Seeds are different from each other. But they are alike in one important way. All seeds need space and light. These allow seeds to take root and grow into adult plants.

Often, a seed cannot find enough space or light near its parent plant. That's why so many seeds are made to travel. Traveling seeds search out new homes where they can grow without as much competition from other plants.

*Dandelion*

*Thistle*

Some seeds fly.

Have you ever blown on a dandelion? A cattail? Seeds from these plants fly using a built-in parachute. It's made up of silky threads that hold the seed aloft even in a light breeze. Then, at some point in its journey, the seed floats to the ground.

*Milkweed*

*Salsify*

*Silver maple*

Other seeds fly using wings.

The wing of the maple seed makes it look like an exotic insect. This wing is a dry, brown husk shaped like a propeller blade. The blade allows the maple seed to twist and turn as it is carried along in the wind.

The fringepod seed has a wing, too. But instead of a large propeller off to one side, it has a small, thin wing circling the entire seed. The fringepod seed can fly a short distance from the parent plant, almost like a paper airplane.

Plants that live near streams, rivers, and oceans often have seeds that swim. These seeds have natural air-pockets inside that act as life jackets.

*Fringepod*

*Maple and elm seeds*

The coconut is an example of a seed made for long-distance swimming. It has a thick coat of tough fibers. It also has a hard shell that makes it airtight and protects it from the harsh ocean water. Inside is the large air-pocket that allows it to float. This unusual seed can swim thousands of miles from its home in Central America to islands in the Pacific Ocean.

*Sprouted coconut*

Many seeds are carried to new places by birds and other animals.

Seeds collected for food are not always eaten. Woodpeckers stash seeds in holes they've drilled in tree trunks. Squirrels and chipmunks play hide-and-seek with acorns, hazelnuts, and hickory nuts. Sometimes the animals forget where these nuts are hidden. Such buried treasures can sprout into large trees and even create whole new forests.

*Acorns stashed by a woodpecker.*

Birds often collect seeds for other reasons. Willow seeds are light and silky, but strong. They form a perfect building material for hummingbird nests.

*Willow seeds*

*Hummingbird*

*Cocklebur seeds*

Some seeds hitchhike.

Cockleburs and Spanish needles have sharp hooks and barbs. These seeds get caught in the coats of furry animals, like dogs, sheep, and donkeys. They might even hook onto the side of your tennis shoe! After hitching a ride, the seeds fall to the ground. There they can take root.

*Spiny hedge parsley and grass seeds in dog's fur*

A few of the hitchhiking seeds can even plant themselves. Filaree seeds grow in groups of five. As they turn brown, their arms spiral outward to form the shape of a pinwheel. The seeds then break off from the group and drop to the ground, where they might snag on an animal's legs.

*Filaree seed group*

After taking a trip, the seed falls to the ground once more. When the rains come, the seed gets wet, and its arm unwinds. Then, as it dries, the arm curls up tightly and drills the seed down into the soil.

*Filaree seed drilling itself into the ground.*

A seed does not need barbs to hitchhike on the back of a friend. Sticky seeds, like mustard, cling to the feet and feathers of birds. Boerhavia seeds can soar for miles by sticking to the breast feathers of tropical birds.

*Boerhavia seeds hitching a ride.*

Many seeds hitchhike on the outside of animals. But there are some seeds that do their traveling on the inside.

Animals like to eat fruits and plants. These foods often contain seeds. The juicy parts of the fruit or plant are digested while the seeds pass right through. Seeds can then take root where they drop. Raspberry, cherry, and mistletoe are just a few of the seeds that travel in this way.

*Mistletoe*

*Mistletoe seeds*

Even tiny insects help seeds hitchhike. Ants especially like trillium seeds. On the side of each seed is a sweet "candy" made of fat. The ant often carries this treat to a new place. There, it eats the candy and leaves the seed along the trail.

There is one other, very odd way that seeds travel. Some seeds explode! It's as if they were shot from a cannon.

*Ant carrying trillium seed.*

*Fat "candies" on trillium seeds*

When certain seed pods and seed holders dry out, they snap — or *catapult* — their seeds into the air. Bean and pea pods, witch hazel and wild geraniums all have seeds that explode. The seeds are then tossed into the air in all directions. Walking through a field of lupine, you can be hit in the face by exploding seeds!

*Lupine*

*Wild geranium*

Seeds that fly. Seeds that swim. Seeds that hitchhike. Seeds that explode.

Just look around you. Traveling seeds are everywhere. You can see them on a walk in the countryside. You will find them on a tropical island or in a bustling city. You may even stumble across them in your own backyard.

Almost anywhere you look, you can see the results of nature's journey — seeds that travel.

Imagine that!

*Witch hazel*

## What Does It Mean?

**barb:** a sharp point that sticks out near the end of a needle, making it hard to pull out

**bustling:** full of busy movement

**competition:** struggle between things

**digest:** to send through the stomach

**exotic:** strange or unusual

**fiber:** a thread

**hitchhike:** to get a free ride

**lush:** healthy, green, and full

**propeller:** blades that turn in circles to move a plane or ship forward

## How Do You Say It?

**boerhavia:** burr HAY vee uh

**filaree:** FILL er ee

**fringepod:** FRINJ pahd

**geranium:** JERR ay nee um

**lupine:** LOO pin

**mistletoe:** MISS ul toe

# I Am the
# FOREST

by YVONNE MARTIN

*If you need help
with hard words,
please turn to p. 66.*

PHOTOGRAPHS:

David Cavagnaro     46-53, 61-62, 66
Stephen McBrady     Cover, title, 39-45, 54-58, 63, 65

ILLUSTRATIONS: Joel Snyder

BOTANICAL CONSULTANT: David Cavagnaro

I cover almost one-third of the earth. I give shelter and warmth to people of all nations. I help supply the water you drink and the fresh air you breathe. To those who seek it, I offer beauty and a peaceful resting place.

I am the forest.

You may think of me as a still, silent stand of trees in the distance. But come closer.

I am more than just trees. I'm a vast, living machine — an *ecosystem*. I'm made up of plants, animals, climate, and soil. The way these parts work together is my *ecology.*

Within my borders you will find five layers of plant life. Each is a neighborhood of its own. And each has a different climate.

The top layer is the *canopy.* It is formed by the tops of my tallest trees. The canopy collects sunlight. It acts as an umbrella to the rest of the forest.

If the canopy is thick and heavy, it will block out the light. Then very little can grow beneath it. If the canopy is thin and airy, light will pass through. Then there will be plenty of growth below.

*Canopy*

In the shade of my canopy you'll find an *understory*. This is made up of trees that like cool places. Many of these trees are young. Over time, it's possible for them to grow taller than the older trees. Then a new, higher canopy is formed.

*Understory*

I Am the Forest

*Shrub layer*

Beneath the understory lies the *shrub layer.* Shrubs are like trees in some ways. But they are bushy, with several small stems instead of one large trunk.

*Herb layer*

Closer to the ground is the beautiful *herb layer.* This is where you'll find many of the brightly-colored, flowering plants of the forest. The herb layer is made up of ferns, grasses, wildflowers, and other plants with soft stems.

*Forest floor*

The ground itself, or *forest floor,* is the final layer. Its cool, solid surface is scattered with dead leaves and twigs. These come from the canopy, understory, shrub and herb layers.

The most important part of the forest floor is something you can't see, because it lies beneath the surface. This is the soil. Soil is formed when bits of rock mix with matter from dead plants and animals. Without it, all the layers of plant life would wither and die.

*Beetle on meadow foam flower*

*Beneath the forest floor*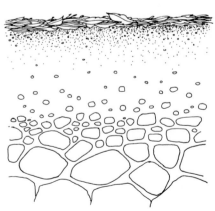

I may be restful, but I'm not at rest. Among the five layers of plants, you'll find constant activity. That's because insects, birds, and other animals play an important role in my ecosystem. They are part of a cycle of life called the *food chain*. As in any chain, each link depends on the other links.

*Crab spider*

The food chain starts with trees and other green plants. These combine sunlight and water with elements from the soil to make food. The food, stored in leaves, branches, nuts, berries, and flowers, is a tasty treat for the animals that live within my borders.

*The food chain*

*Monarch butterfly*

Insects eat green leaves and roots. They drink the sap of wildflowers. Birds search for seeds. Chipmunks and tree squirrels scurry from limb to limb, looking for acorns to eat or store.

There are even foods for larger animals. The yellow-bellied marmot uses its front teeth to chew on the soft inner bark of my trees. Bears lumber across my floor in search of nuts, berries, and roots.

*Chipmunk*

*Yellow-bellied marmot*

*Black bear*

The food chain continues as other creatures in my kingdom hunt plant-eating animals.

Bulgy-eyed frogs use long, quick tongues to pick insects off plants. Great horned owls swoop down in the dark of night to catch rodents and frogs. The fox's meals are made up of birds and other small animals.

*Yellow-legged frog*

*Great horned owl*

*Red fox*

*Bacteria breaking down fallen tree trunk*

The food chain is completed by tiny living things called *bacteria*. After plants and animals die, the bacteria work to break them down. What is left can once again be used by trees and green plants to make food.

I am very old. But parts of me are being born each day. Though single trees may die, new seedlings spring up to fill the gaps. Even after a flood or forest fire, I live on. Seeds left behind sprout and work to build up what has been destroyed.

As parts of me grow, I grow, too. The grassy meadows around me provide the perfect home for my seeds, which are looking for space and

light. The seeds sprout. New trees and plants take hold. Over time, I stretch my borders into the meadow.

Each part of my ecosystem depends on another part. And whether you know it, you depend on me.

My trees are your source of shelter and warmth. They provide wood to build houses. They fuel the blaze in your fireplace. They were even used to make the paper these words are printed on.

My trees work to prevent floods. The leaves and branches slow the rain. The soil beneath acts as a giant sponge. And the roots hold the soil in place.

In the high mountains, the shade I provide keeps the snow from melting too fast. Instead, it melts slowly during the spring and summer months. In this way, I keep lakes and streams filled with fresh water through the year.

I help make fresh air. While my trees are turning sunlight into food, they give off the oxygen you breathe.

I give you a place to enjoy nature. You might come to fish, picnic, hike, or camp. You might come just to see my plants and animals.

People depend on me. But sometimes they are my enemy.

People cause pollution. Chemicals released into the air and water can harm my plant and animal life. Trash left behind by thoughtless visitors is another kind of pollution. Litter makes a visit less enjoyable for others who follow.

Though they may not mean to, people cause nine out of ten forest fires. Some fires start when a lit cigarette is thrown from a car. Other fires begin when hot embers are left in a campfire. Such careless mistakes can create a blaze that will destroy my carefully balanced ecosystem.

I am the forest. Just as plants and animals are part of my life, I am part of yours. I am strong, but I am not forever.

Please, take care of me.

## *What Does It Mean?*

**destroy:** to kill or ruin

**gap:** a space between things

**litter:** trash

**shelter:** a protected place

**stem:** the main trunk of a plant

**supply:** to give or provide

**twig:** a small branch

**wither:** to dry up

## *How Do You Say It?*

**beauty:** BEW tee

**chemical:** KEM ih cull

**climate:** CLY mut

**ecology:** ih CALL uh jee

**ecosystem:** EE ko sis tum

**herb:** ERB

**marmot:** MAR mut

**sponge:** SPUNJ

**tongue:** TUNG

# Big Red

by MELINDA TERRY

*If you need help*
*with hard words,*
*please turn to p. 96.*

PHOTOGRAPHS: Stephen McBrady
ILLUSTRATIONS: Joel Snyder
*We gratefully acknowledge the cooperation of Ralph's Grocery Company.*

My name is Erica, but the kids at school call me Big Red.

It's not because of the way I look. I'm not big and I don't have red hair. They call me Big Red because I grow big red tomatoes in my own backyard.

It all started one night at dinner. My dad had cooked a plate of hamburgers.

Looking for things to put on the bun, I saw lettuce. I saw pickles and onion slices. I saw mustard and ketchup. But I didn't see my favorite food — tomatoes.

Dad said the tomatoes at the store weren't very good during the early spring months. Then he told me about the delicious tomatoes he had grown at home when he was young.

"Those tomatoes were the best," he said. "They were full of flavor. The great thing was that you could pick a big, juicy tomato from the vine and eat it while it was still warm from the summer sun."

Then and there, I decided to grow my very
own tomatoes in the backyard. The next time
Dad cooked hamburgers, I would just reach
down and pick a tomato right off the vine.

Later that week I went to see Mrs. Thompson,
the owner of our local nursery.

"What kind of tomatoes do you have in
mind?" she asked. "They come in different
shapes and sizes."

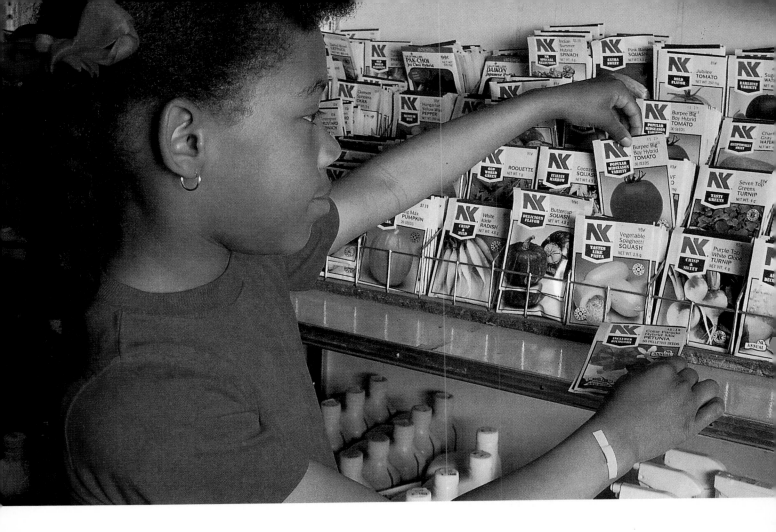

I considered cherry tomatoes, which are small and bite-size. I thought about plum tomatoes, shaped like pears. Finally I decided on good old-fashioned beefsteak tomatoes. Those are the ones that are big, red, and round.

*Beefsteak tomato,*
*plum tomato,*
*cherry tomatoes*

I found a sunny spot in our backyard. Before starting to work, I gathered all the tools I would need to build my tomato patch. I also had a library book on gardening.

Using red yarn tied to four small stakes, I marked off a square. I prepared the soil inside the square, making sure it was soft without too many lumps. Then I mixed in compost, so the plants would have good food while they were growing.

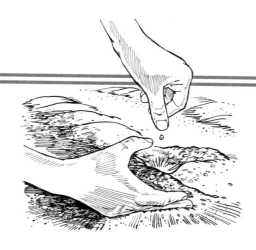

I moved the yarn to mark two straight rows, about twenty-four inches apart. Every two inches I dropped a seed and covered it up. Drop and cover. Drop and cover. Before long, both rows were done.

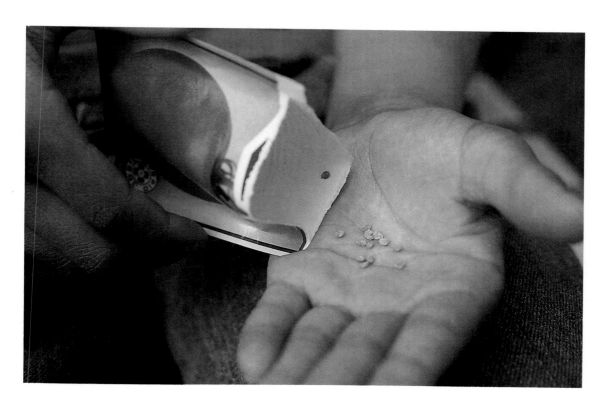

As a final touch, I planted flower seeds along the edges of the tomato patch to make a colorful border.

Before going in for dinner, I watered my garden. The light shower from a watering can was better for the seeds than drowning them with our garden hose.

Each day that week, I couldn't wait to get

home from school to check on my tomato plants. I watered them. I wiggled my toes in the moist, cool dirt. Most of the time, though, I just watched and waited for something to happen.

My dad seemed to know what I was thinking. "Don't worry," he said. "Once those plants start, they'll grow fast, like Jack's beanstalk. You'll see."

He was right. About two weeks later, little green sprouts appeared. Soon they were over six inches high. Now I had real tomato plants that I could call my own.

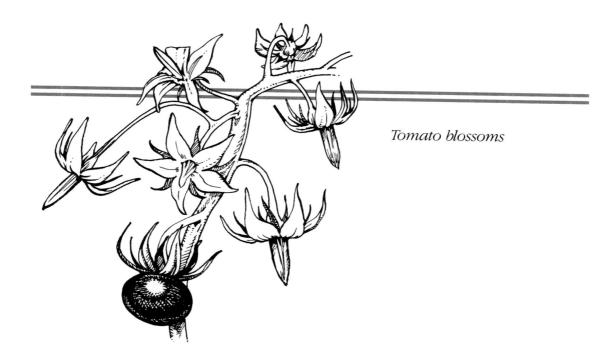

*Tomato blossoms*

The plants were fun to look at and touch. Each had a long center stem that stood straight up. The branches held lots of bumpy, fuzzy leaves with pointed edges.

That weekend, I picked out the strongest plants and pulled the rest. I hated to do it, but I had to make room for the healthiest ones to grow.

One night, Dad woke me up after I had fallen asleep. "Erica," he said, "it's going to be cold tonight. We need to cover your tomato plants so they won't freeze."

I put on some shoes, and together we tiptoed into the night to cover the seedlings with a sheet.

The plants survived the late spring frost. I kept watering and feeding them. They kept

growing. Finally, when they were about fifteen inches high, they started drooping under their own weight. I tied each one to a tall stake to hold it up straight.

The plants looked good. There was just one problem. I still didn't have a single tomato.

I have to admit, I was worried. If I couldn't grow one tomato, how could people grow the hundreds I saw each week in the supermarket?

That Saturday I went straight to the produce section at our store. I told the produce man about my tomato patch and asked if he had any advice.

"Tomatoes take time," he said. "It's a full three months between planting and the first harvest."

When I asked him to tell me about it, he explained that commercial tomatoes are grown in fields stretching as far as the eye can see. The tomatoes range from red to green when they're taken from the vine.

After being picked, they are placed in large bins and hauled to a packing plant. There the tomatoes are put onto a moving conveyor belt and washed. That's when the sorting begins.

The first sort is for quality. Tomatoes that aren't good enough for the produce section are taken out. These are used to make relishes and other canned and bottled products.

Next an electronic eye sorts the tomatoes by color. The red tomatoes are for nearby stores.

The greener ones are shipped across the country, so they can ripen on the way.

Finally the tomatoes are sorted by size. The big tomatoes are dropped down one chute and the smaller ones down another.

The last step is to hand-pack tomatoes of the same color and size into shipping cartons. The boxes are stapled shut and stacked, then loaded onto trucks and taken to supermarkets.

I looked at the tomatoes in the store display. "Boy," I said, "I wish I had a few of these growing in my garden."

"You will," he said. "Just be patient."

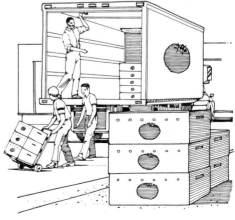

Then it happened. One morning I went out to the backyard to check my plants. Like Christmas trees, each of them had sprouted tiny green ornaments!

The next few weeks passed quickly. Each day brought new tomatoes. And the ones already on the vine kept getting bigger. Some were starting to turn red.

One night, my mom said we were all going to go out for dinner at a fancy new restaurant. "Let's catch up with your dad out in the garage," she said.

But Dad wasn't in the garage. He was standing by the barbecue, holding a plate filled with tomatoes from my garden.

"Surprise!" he said. "Welcome to the Ritz Backyard Grill, home of the world's best tomatoes."

Finally! My tomato patch was a success. And my hamburger was complete at last.

## What Does It Mean?

**commercial:** meant to be sold

**compost:** a kind of fertilizer that helps make plants grow

**conveyer belt:** a moving belt that carries things

**electronic eye:** a machine that can "see" movement or color

**harvest:** the time when crops are picked

**nursery:** a store where plants are sold

**produce section:** the part of a supermarket where fruits and vegetables are sold

**supermarket:** a large food store

## How Do You Say It?

**chute:** SHOOT

**commercial:** kuh MER shul

**compost:** CAHM post

**conveyer:** kun VAY er

**electronic:** ih lek TRAHN ik

**produce:** PRO doos